I. INTRODUCTION

It has long been suspected by lawyers and economists that firms may use the unfair trade laws, primarily antidumping (AD), to foster collusive agreements between firms. (Calvani et al. (1986) and Prusa (1992)) This collusion may either be among domestic firms or between domestic and foreign firms. For example, a domestic firm or industry may file an AD petition containing incorrect information and fraudulently obtain dumping relief, effectively removing import competition. A domestic firm or firms may also abuse the unfair trade laws by using them as a threat to negotiate a collusive agreement with a foreign competitor. Anecdotal evidence suggests that suspicion of these types of abuses are not unfounded.

In 1989, the largest U.S. based producers of ferrosilicon, an industrial metal, formed a cartel, set a collusive price and withdrew capacity from the market. These firms then used the drop in their sales to prove injury from dumping and AD duties were imposed in 1993 against five foreign competitors. The U.S. firms were then free to manage the cartel. When imports began to enter the United States from another country, Brazil, the U.S. firms invited the Brazilians to enter the cartel. The Brazilian producers did not accept the offer and were then subject to an AD claim and duties were imposed. Eventually the cartel was discovered and cartel members have been found guilty in both criminal and civil proceedings (USITC (1999a) Pierce (2000)). These series of events provide an example of the use of the AD process to exclude foreign competition and to attempt to entice/coerce them into collusive agreements.

Other anecdotal evidence suggest that this is not an isolated incident. In a 1995 district court case (Music Center v. Prestini Musical Instrument Company, 874 F. Supp. 543 E.D. NY 1995), it was alleged by the foreign firm in the complaint that the domestic firm made an offer to collude with the threat of an AD claim if the overture was rejected. It was alleged that the refusal of the foreign firm triggered the AD complaint. The court did not rule on the merits of this invitation to collude claim since the foreign firm had not alleged that they were injured.

There is a belief in the economics literature that a withdrawn AD petition is a signal that foreign and domestic firms have reached a collusive out-of-court settlement. This hypothesis was first suggest and investigated by Prusa (1992) and later cited by other economists. (Rosendorff (1996) & Zanardi (2000)). This belief is questionable. While there have been studies on the economic effects of AD cases in which duties were imposed, truly withdrawn cases, cases where the domestic firms withdraw the petition without a government negotiated settlement, have not received the same degree of attention. This paper will examine whether trade data supports the belief that withdrawn petitions precede decreases in quantity or increases in the price of subject imports, i.e. a collusive settlement.

The potential collusive effects of withdrawn AD petitions is an important research question for a number of reason. Gallaway et al (1999) estimate that the combined effect of the AD and countervailing (CVD) laws had a negative effect on the U.S. economy of four billion dollars in 1993. This effect is only for cases where duties were imposed. Since only approximately one-half of cases end in duties and approximately 10 percent of cases are withdrawn without a known settlement, if withdrawn cases have a welfare effect, they should be included in the overall economic impact of the unfair trade remedy laws.

There is also a belief that collusive settlements to AD complainants resulting in withdrawn petitions are legal as well as common (Prusa (1992)). While this paper does not offer an in-depth legal analysis of whether an out-of-court settlement to an AD complaint is legal, this issue is discussed. While there is limited case law on the subject, a settlement of an AD case which affects the price and/or quantity of subject imports, not involving a joint venture, is illegal. From an antitrust perspective, if settlements exist they need to be investigated.

The purpose of this paper is to examine the effects of unfair trade cases (AD/CVD) that are withdrawn by petitioners. The effects examined are the price and quantity changes associated with the investigations on subject imports. In contrast to most of the previous research in this area, we use detailed product level quantity and unit value data and only examine truly withdrawn cases and find that most withdrawn cases either have a procompetitive effect, i.e. prices decrease or quantities increase after the petition is withdrawn, or they have no effect. In a few cases the quantity and price changes after the cases are withdrawn are not inconsistent with an anticompetitive settlement.

To understand the institutional background and to motivate the empirical specification that follows, Section II presents a description of the AD process and the legal aspects of an out-of-court settlement. Section III contains a review of previous research on the topics covered in this paper. Section IV discusses the methodology and data that are used in the estimation process. Section V discusses the results of the empirical estimation. Section VI concludes with discussions of the policy implications of the results and avenues for further research in this area.

II. U.S. AD/CVD Procedure and Settlement Antitrust Implications[1]

To motivate the empirical specification and ease the discussion of previous research it is important to briefly summarize the process by which U.S. AD complaints are investigated. The AD process starts with petitions being simultaneously filed at both the Commerce Department's International Trade Administration (ITA) and the U.S. International Trade Commission (ITC). The ITA determines whether the foreign product is being sold at less than fair value (LTFV)[2] in the United States. The ITC determines whether the domestic industry has been injured by sales at LTFV. This is a multi-step process in which both agencies make preliminary and final determinations. Full investigations take approximately one year if they continue to completion, but the investigation may be terminated prior to completion by a negative decision, a withdrawn petition, or a suspension agreement. It is very important to distinguish between the reasons that a case does not continue until a final injury determination. In some of the research in this area suspended and withdrawn of cases have been treated as if they were the same and combined for estimation purposes. (Prusa (1999)) In a pooled estimation of the effects of suspended and withdrawn cases this could lead to finding an effect from withdrawn cases that may not exist.

---

[1] For a more detailed description of the AD/CVD process see USITC (1995) Chapter 2 or USITC (1999b).

[2] "Fair" or "normal" value is based on home market sales. If home market sales are not available, third country markets prices or constructed values are used.

Within 20 days of the petition's filing, the ITA must determine whether the petition is in order. Within 25 days of receiving notification from ITA, the ITC must determine if there is a "reasonable indication" that an industry in the United States is materially injured, threatened with material injury, or the establishment of the industry in the United States is materially retarded by reason of LTFV imports of the subject product.[3]

After an affirmative decision by the ITC, the ITA has 140 days from the filing of the petition to determine whether there is a reasonable basis to believe that the product in question was sold or is likely to be sold at LTFV. The ITA calculates a preliminary dumping margin for individual firms being investigated and an 'all other' margin for the remaining firms. Once ITA makes an affirmative determination, a duty based on the AD margins must be paid on imports of the subject merchandise. These duties, which may be posted as bonds, are held pending the outcome of the rest of the investigation. If ITA's preliminary decision is negative, no duty is required, but the investigation continues.

Within 235 days of the filing of the petition, ITA must make its final determination of sales at LTFV, and calculate the final AD margins. If ITA's final determination is affirmative, it instructs the U.S. Customs Service (Customs) to continue collecting duties. If ITA's final decision is negative, the investigation ends and Customs stops collecting the duty and refunds all deposits that have been paid with interest.

The ITC must make a final determination within 120 days of ITA's affirmative preliminary decision and 45 days after ITA's affirmative final decision. As in the preliminary determination, the ITC determines whether there is material injury or threat of injury, but no longer uses the reasonable indication criteria. If the ITC determination is negative, the ITA informs Customs to stop collecting duties on the product and to refund all previously collected duties, with interest. If the ITC's determination is affirmative, it also has to determine whether

---

[3] The U.S. AD law defines material injury as "harm which is not inconsequential, immaterial or unimportant". 19 U.S.C. 1667 (7)(A).

duties should have been collected from the point at which they were initially imposed or from the time of the final ITC determination.

At any point after the ITA preliminary determination and prior to the ITC's final determination, the investigation may be withdrawn or suspended. Suspension occurs if the ITA reaches an agreement with the foreign firms to stop the LTFV sales to the U.S. market either by a cessation of sales to the U.S. or by raising their prices. If the petition is withdrawn by the petitioner, the investigation will end with the concurrence of the ITA.

An important legal question, concerning withdrawn petitions, is to what extent a private out of court settlement between foreign and domestic firms violates U.S. antitrust laws. There is an antitrust doctrine, referred to as Noerr-Pennington, which allows firms in the domestic industry to work together and exchange information in order to lobby for government actions, i.e. file an AD complaint. The Noerr-Pennington doctrine establishes the circumstances in which private efforts to elicit anticompetitive government action are immune from antitrust challenges. (American Bar Association (1997))

Prusa (1992, p.7) and subsequent papers assert that, "the Noerr-Pennington exemption broadens the scope for relief and allows the domestic industry to withdraw its petition after achieving a settlement." The government guidelines on U.S. antitrust policy and limited court cases suggest that this is not true.

The Antitrust Enforcement Guidelines for International Operations issued by the U.S. Department of Justice and the Federal Trade Commission, clearly address this issue (U.S. DOJ, 1995). A genuine effort to obtain or influence government action is immune from the Sherman Act. For example if domestic firms exchange competitive information in order to file an AD claim, this would be protected by Noerr-Pennington as long as the exchanges are reasonably necessary to file the petition. However, the examples and discussion point out that a private agreement between U.S. and foreign firms affecting prices or quantities without the involvement of the ITA, i.e. a suspension agreement, would be illegal.

> In certain instances, the U.S. trade laws set forth specific procedures for settling disputes under those laws, which can involve price and quantity agreement by the foreign firms

involved. When those procedures are followed, an implied antitrust immunity results. However agreements among competitors that do not comply with the law, or go beyond the measures authorized by the law, do not enjoy antitrust immunity. (U.S. DOJ 1995 - Section 3.4)

An example of a legal case very similar to the situation of a withdrawn AD petition was United States v. Nat'l Board of Fur Farms Orgs., 395 F. Supp. 56 (E.D. Wis. 1975) and the subsequent settlement. In this case domestic mink farmers participated in an agreement whereby they would abandon their attempts to secure import relief from the U.S. government in exchange for price fixing with foreign competitors. The Justice Department prosecuted and reached a settlement with the domestic mink farmers that they would cease and desist (Calvani et al (1986)). Even though there is little precedent on this type of case, it is clear that a private settlement of an AD dispute which attempted to increase prices or decrease imports without some other rational, such as a joint venture, would be illegal.

III. REVIEW OF PREVIOUS LITERATURE

There have been a number of investigations of the many facets of AD cases. Several articles have focused on the effects of AD duties on imports to the U.S. and on domestic output (See Kalt (1988), and Morkre and Kelly (1994)). Only a few articles have touched upon the main topic of this paper, the effects on subject import price and quantity due to a withdrawn case. There are more articles which look whether there is an effect of the investigation. The research pertaining to these topics are summarized below and can be classified into several categories by the methodology used. These categories are game theoretic with empirical support, and econometric.

Prusa (1992) presents a game theoretic bargaining model where a domestic firm and a foreign firm compete in prices and shows that they will prefer a settlement to duties and therefore there is an incentive to withdraw cases. Prusa examines the value of trade both before and after the petition is filed in AD cases. This is done on an aggregate basis of all cases for the two years, 1980-1981, and he looks at ratios of the value traded to detect changes in response to investigations. By examining the data in this way, Prusa concludes that the filing of the petition has no effect on the value of imports. However, once the petition is accepted he concludes it does not matter whether duties are imposed or a settlement is reached, the effects are the same. One interpretation of the model results is that AD petitions serve as a basis to achieve a cooperative level of profits for the foreign and domestic firms. In other words the AD process may allow foreign and domestic competitors to negotiate a settlement that benefits both of them.

An extension to Prusa's model is given in Zanardi (2000). In his model he examines when the domestic firm should withdraw a petition and reach a collusive out of court settlement with the foreign firm. A shortcoming of the Prusa model is that it predicts that all cases should be settled. Prusa's model is a special case of the more general Zanardi model. Zanardi also constructs a dataset to measure domestic firm's and foreign firm's coordination costs and bargaining power. Since the measures of relative coordination costs and bargaining power support the theoretical predictions of the model, he concludes that this is consistent with the hypotheses that AD law is used as a collusive device with respect to withdrawn petitions.

An early attempt to econometrically test the effect of affirmative AD investigations on foreign firms is Herander and Schwartz (1984). They examine the dumping margins of foreign firms during 1976-1981 to see if the threat of an AD investigation affects the margins or duty rates of subsequent AD cases. In other words do previous AD cases in a given industry cause foreign firms in that industry to raise their prices to head off future cases. They find that higher probabilities of a petition in a given industry reduce the margins found in that industry when other cases are filed previously. In other words, the threat of an AD investigation raises prices.

Harrison (1991) uses quarterly SITC data on 41 product categories to examine the effect of AD duties on import prices. She tests for the impact of investigations as well as the duties themselves. The OLS results show that investigations have mixed results on the prices, whereas AD duties should raise import prices. When accounting for the simultaneity problem of prices and duties, the results are inconclusive with respect to both investigations and the imposition of duties. So in both specifications there is no investigation effect.

Staiger and Wolak (1994) develop a dataset for AD cases for 1980-85. They use annual import data aggregated to the 4-digit SIC level to look at the effects of AD on the value of subject imports as well as on output in the domestic industry. Since their import data are on an annual basis, and since AD cases last less than a year and may overlap calendar years, they construct an index of the number of AD cases within the industry for each year. They use the change in this index to judge the effects of the AD investigation process on imports and domestic output. Their model shows that the imposition of an AD duty on a single tariff line will generate a drop in annual imports of 10.55 million 1972 dollars. They find substantial investigative effects with a drop in subject imports of approximately 50 percent in the period after the case is filed. However they find no evidence of an impact in imports of a withdrawn case. Cases that ended with suspension agreements have about half the effect as those where AD duties were imposed in their dataset.

USITC (1995) evaluates the impact of AD orders focusing on 8 products where AD orders were imposed. Each case study econometrically analyzes the impact of the AD duties on imports and prices. Estimations are done on a quarterly basis based on a system of equations looking at the supply and demand of the domestic and foreign products. In 3 of the 8 cases a significant drop in import quantity occurs during the investigation period.

Krupp and Pollard (1996) examine all AD cases in the chemical industry from 1976 to 1988. The main strength of this paper is that it uses disaggregated trade data to examine the effects of these cases. A simple one equation market model relates import revenue to a number of variables including the timing of the investigation and duty imposition. They find investigation effects for most of the cases. They only have one withdrawn case in their sample. This case was withdrawn after a suspension agreement, which had the expect effect of reducing the value of imports.

Prusa (1999) uses annual data on the value, quantity and unit value of imports to examine the effects of AD investigations on trade. The cases are classified as affirmative, where duties are imposed, negative, where there was a negative final injury determination, and settled. Settled cases include those that end in a suspension agreement, a voluntary restraint agreement, or the withdrawal of the petition. He finds significant reductions in trade for affirmative and settled cases. There are stronger quantity effects than price effects. The reduction in the quantity of trade is similar for the settled cases and the affirmative cases. Prices increase less when cases are settled than when duties are imposed. However, settled cases include both suspended cases where a settlement has been reached and withdrawn cases where a settlement may or may not exist. In grouping these cases together, the estimated effect off this collection of cases is a weighted average of the suspended and withdrawn cases. Since there were settlements in the suspended cases that should have limited imports, the weighted average effect of all the suspended and withdrawn cases says nothing about the effects of withdrawn cases.

A slightly different econometric approach to examine the effect of investigations or the imposition of duties is an event study. An event such as an AD petition filing or the imposition of AD duties is examined using time series data before, during, and after the event. Hartigan et al (1986, 1989) and Lenway et al. (1990) examine the impact of trade measures on market returns to firms that are affected by AD investigations. Most relevant for this paper is Hartigan et al. (1989), which analyzes the effects of the investigation process by evaluating the return to the stock verses the expected return of companies who were judged to be affected by AD cases. Firms are found to gain during the investigation process even when the outcome is negative, i.e. no duties are imposed. This implies that import quantities, prices or both should be affected as a result of an investigation or settlement. Their analysis does not allow the price and quantity effects to be identified.

The present paper is the only one that examines a dataset based exclusively on withdrawn petitions. In addition, much of the previous research in this area uses aggregate data. Much of this research uses annual data, on an SIC or SITC basis, and this data measures the value of imports from all countries. The data on the cases in this paper shows an average 30 percent market share of subject imports to total imports at the 10-digit harmonized tariff schedule (HTS) level of disaggregation. Much of the previous research did not break out subject and non-subject imports when examining antidumping cases. Aggregating to SIC or SITC level may likewise obscure effects of the AD process. Since the investigation process takes less than a year, using annual data to analyze the effects of the investigation process is tenuous, at best.

A more important weakness is the use of value import data rather than import quantities and prices or unit values. Because the expected effects of AD investigations includes rising import prices and falling quantities, outcomes in terms of import values may be inconclusive. In fact, results showing that AD investigations have a positive, negative, or no effect would be possible under a plausible range of elasticity values for the demand for imports. Hence, research using import values that find no effects of the AD process is not surprising and should not be taken as strong evidence that these results do not exist.

IV. DESCRIPTION OF METHODOLOGY AND DATA

A. Methodology

The main hypothesis tested is whether the withdrawal of an AD/CVD petition leads to an increase in the price and/or decrease in the quantity of the imports subject to investigation. These types of price movements would be consistent with a collusive out-of-court settlement being reached. This is the general belief put forth in Prusa (1992) and cited by others that a withdrawn petition signals such an agreement. A related question is whether the data show an investigation effect, i.e., does the quantity of imports decrease or price increase between the filing of the petition and its withdrawal. It is also important to examine the reaction of imports from countries not subject to the investigation as well. In much of the literature one of the main effects found from the unfair trade laws is trade diversion (Messerlin (1989), Prusa (1997) and Krupp & Pollard (1996)). In the ferrosilicon case, the main trade effect was a decrease in the quantity from the countries subject to the duties and an increase from non-subject countries. In that case the colluding firms increased their supply to the United States from their foreign operations.

As a first pass a simple regression of the value, quantity and price (unit value) of the subject imports were regressed on dummy variables for the 12 months before the petition filing, the months during the investigation, and the 12 months after the case was withdrawn. The value, quantity, and price regressions are equations (1), (2), and (3) respectively. These regressions are a more refined version of the ratios calculated in Prusa (1992) and similar to the regressions in Prusa (1999).

$$Ln(P*Q_s) = \beta_0 AD_2 + \beta_1 AD_3 + \beta_2 AD_4 + \epsilon \tag{1}$$

$Ln(P*Q_s)$ = Value of Subject Imports
AD_2 = Dummy 12 Months before Petition Filing
AD_3 = Dummy Investigation
AD_4 = Dummy 12 Months after Withdrawn Petition before Petition Filing

$$Ln(Q_s) = \beta_0 AD_2 + \beta_1 AD_3 + \beta_2 AD_4 + \epsilon \tag{2}$$

$Ln(Q_s)$ = Quantity of Subject Imports

$$Ln(P_s) = \beta_0 AD_2 + \beta_1 AD_3 + \beta_2 AD_4 + \epsilon \tag{3}$$

$Ln(P_s)$ = Price of Subject Imports

The data, as described below, is monthly from 1989-1998. The 120 observation are divided into 5 periods. Period 1 is from 1990 until 12 months before the AD petition is filed, AD_1. Period 2 is the 12 months prior to the petition being filed, AD_2. Period 3 is during the investigation, AD_3. Period 4 is the 12 months after the petition is withdrawn, AD_4. Period 5 is the 13th month after the petition is withdrawn until the end of the dataset, AD_5. These equations are estimated both cases by case and pooled with case fixed effects.

To more thoroughly analyze the effects of withdrawn petitions, a more fully specified system of interactions is estimated. In order to estimate a separate price and quantity effect of withdrawn petitions on subject imports, and to control for the other imports, a system of demand and supply equations were estimated. A three equation system with an inverse demand for subject imports, a supply of subject imports and a demand for rest of world imports comprise the system. The constant elasticity supply and demand framework is given below. For examples of simultaneous demand-supply systems for international trade see Golstein and Khan (1978) and Carey (1997).

$$\ln(P_S) = \beta_0 + \beta_1 Ln(Q_S) + \beta_2 \ln(P_{NS}) + \beta_3 Ln(P_{U.S.}) + \beta_4 \ln(Y_{U.S.}) + \beta_5(AD_2) + \beta_6(AD_3) + \beta_7(AD_4) + \beta_8(AD_5) + \epsilon \quad (4)$$

Equation four is the inverse demand equation for subject imports. The variables are the unit value of subject imports, P_s, the quantity of subject imports, Q_s, the price of non-subject imports, P_{NS}, the producer price index, $P_{U.S.}$, U.S. industrial production, $Y_{U.S.}$, and the dummy variable for the five time periods one-year before filing, AD_2, during the investigation, AD_3, one-year after the withdrawal, AD_4, and from one-year after withdrawal until the end of the dataset, AD_5.

Equation five is the supply curve for subject imports. The additional variables are exchange rates, ExR_s, and industrial production of the subject country, O_s. Equations 4 and 5

$$\ln(Q_S) = \alpha_0 + \alpha_1 \ln(P_S) + \alpha_2 \ln(ExR_S) + \alpha_3 \ln(O_S) + \alpha_4(AD_2) + \alpha_5(AD_3)\alpha_6(AD_4)\alpha_7(AD_5) + \epsilon \quad (5)$$

comprise the simultaneous system of demand and supply of subject imports. P_s and Q_s are endogenous and the exogenous variables in equations four and five are used as instruments. The demand relationship is identified by the exchange rates and the output in the subject country (Goldberg and Knetter (1999)). The supply equation is identified by the price of the non-subject imports, and the price level and output in the United States.

$$\ln(Q_{NS}) = \gamma_0 + \gamma_1 \ln(P_{NS}) + \gamma_2 \ln(P_S) + \gamma_3 \ln(P_{U.S.}) + \gamma_4 \ln(Y_{U.S.}) + \gamma_5(AD_2) + \gamma_6(AD_3) + \gamma_7(AD_4) + \gamma_8(AD_5) + \epsilon \quad (6)$$

Equation six is the demand curve for rest of world imports, Q_{NS}. The supply of rest of world imports is assumed to be perfectly elastic. (Thursby and Thursby, 1984) In most cases there are multiple country supply the United States that are not subject to investigation.

This system was estimated using three stage least squares. This estimation technique allows for correlation across the error terms and helps mitigate possible omitted variable bias. Monthly binary variables were included in all three equations as well to capture seasonal effects.

To make sure that the regressions were not spurious because of non-stationary variables, the augmented Dickey-Fuller test for unit roots was performed. In all cases the dependent variable was I(0). The only independent variable that was I(1) was industrial production. That variable was included in levels as well as first difference. As an additional check for growth trends in the import data, the system was estimated with a time trend in each equation.

B. Data

Between 1990 and 1997 approximately nine percent of all AD and CVD cases were withdrawn without an official settlement, either a suspension agreement or a voluntary export restraint. A little over one percent of the cases ended in some kind of official settlement.[4] In 47 percent of cases duties were imposed following affirmative final determinations by the ITA and the ITC. The remainder were resolved through the normal investigation process in which terminations occur because of negative determinations. Cases are terminated if the ITA reached a negative final determination of sales at LTFV or if the ITC reaches a negative injury determination in either the preliminary stage or the final stage of the investigation. Cases considered in this analysis include only investigations that were withdrawn. Those cases terminated before the final determination are sometime mis-classified as withdrawn. Table I describes the cases analyzed in this paper. The table shows the product, the subject country, the ITC case number, the month the petition was filed and the month it was withdrawn. It is important to point out that most cases are withdrawn relatively quickly. The average number of months a case is under investigation before being withdrawn in this dataset is just under three months. Thirteen of the twenty-one cases were withdrawn in one or two months.[5] This is

---

[4] Other time periods have a greater number of withdrawn cases, see Prusa (1992) and Prusa (1999). In addition it is important to separately count cases that end in an official settlement from those that are withdrawn without a known settlement.

[5] I am counting the cordage cases as four cases instead of twelve. One of the difficulties in counting the number of cases is how to treat a withdrawn and refiled case. The cordage cases

important when considering whether it is likely that a collusive out of court settlement was reached.

Products subject to AD investigations are very narrowly defined. They do not always map to the harmonized tariff schedule (HTS) categories on a one-to-one to basis, but the public record generally includes a list of HTS codes under which the subject imports enter the United States. *Federal Register* notices that announce the initiation, preliminary and final stages of the investigation identify the HTS codes under which subject products are imported. Monthly import values and quantities were obtained for subject imports at the 10-digit HTS level of disaggregation from the January 1989 through December 1998. There were 16 cases that have separate volumes and quantities and five cases that did not. Case specific information on the initiation, termination, and preliminary and final decision dates was also collected.

The five dummy variables divide the dataset into the time leading up to one year before filing, within one year before filing, the investigation, within one year after filing and the period between one year after filing and the end of the data set. The other variables came from the Survey of Current business, (industrial production of the United States and the producer price index), and the International Monetary Fund, (exchange rates and industrial output of the subject country).

One strength of this analysis is the level of detail in the data. By focusing on the subject imports, we are able to better identify the timing effects associated AD investigations. In addition, we are less likely to aggregate imports subject to AD investigations with non-subject imports. The primary weakness of this level of detail is it decreases the ability to match the import data to domestic production and prices. Given the disaggregated nature of the data it is difficult to find other explanatory variables. Domestic price indices are not collected at the same level of detail as the import data, so we are not able to calculate the relative prices of imports to domestic production.

---

were withdrawn and refiled twice.

V. RESULTS

The simple single equations regressions given in equations one through three are estimated to give a benchmark for the more complex system regressions. These simple regressions are a more refined version of the ratios calculated in Prusa (1992) and similar to the regressions in Prusa (1999). For all the cases the monthly value of subject imports was regressed on the binary variables for one year before the petition was filed, the investigation period and the one year after. This was done for the entire set of cases with case fixed effects and then case by case. For the 16 cases which have quantity data, the monthly import quantities and unit values are regressed on the same variables pooled with case fixed effects and then case by case.

The results of these regression are summarized in Tables II and III. The coefficients on the year before and year after variables are presented along with the test of whether the difference in the two coefficients is statistically different from zero. Table II shows the results for aggregate value regression on the 21 cases as a whole with case fixed effects and the results of the individual case regression for the 16 cases with quantity and unit value data. Table III shows the results of the value regressions for those cases with only value data.

Overall, the cases show a statistically significant increase in trade comparing the year before the petition was filed with one year after the petition was withdrawn. The average increase in the value of trade was 21 percent.[6] Ten of the 21 cases showed a statistically significant increase in trade. No case showed a statistically significant decrease in trade. Of the 11 cases that showed no statistical increase in trade, seven showed a statistically insignificant decrease in trade.

For the 16 cases with quantity and unit value data, most showed an increase in the quantity of subject imports. The average increase of all the cases estimated with case fixed effects was 30 percent. Eight cases showed a significant increase in trade, one showed a significant decrease in the quantity of trade and seven showed no significant change. The unit

---

[6]To interpret the dummy variable coefficient (α) as a percent change, $e^{\alpha}-1$, Kennedy (1981).

value regressions showed similar results. The average price decrease for all cases estimated with case fixed effects is 10 percent. Eight cases showed no significant change in the unit value, five showed a decrease in the unit value and three showed a significant increase in unit value.

There is little support, in these simple regressions, for the notion that withdrawn AD and CVD duty petitions are a signal of a collusive agreement between the domestic firms and the foreign firms subject to investigation. There is only one case, steel wire rod from Belgium, case number 686, where quantity dropped and price increased and two cases, bulk ibuprofen from India, case number 526 and ultra high temperature milk from Canada, case number 767, where prices increased after the petitions were withdrawn. It is important to point out that the cases which did show a decrease in quantity or increase in price did not show a significant difference in trade volume. In other words it is important to look at prices and quantities not just the volume of trade. While there is not a great deal of support for the collusive hypothesis in the simple regressions, the simple regressions do not control for a number of important variables in the supply and demand system.

The supply-demand system was estimated case by case. Overall the supply-demand framework fits the data well. In the vast majority of cases the supply and demand curves have the expected slope, the control variables have the right sign and are significant much of the time and the R-squareds are reasonably high. Given the wide variety of effects of the withdrawn cases shown in the simple regressions and the range of coefficients on the case by case regressions for the other explanatory variables, pooling the data was not appropriate.

Table IV presents the coefficients of the dummy variables for one year before, during and one year after the investigation as well as the tests statistics for whether there is a differences in the parameter estimates. Overall the results are very similar to the results of the simple regressions. There are two cases which show a decrease in quantity or an increase in price after a withdrawn petition. These are two of the three cases that had these type of effects in the simple regressions, steel wire rod from Belgium and ultra high temperature milk from Canada.

In most cases there was no significant change in quantities or unit values or the variables moved in a procompetitive direction. Trade with non-subject countries in about half the cases increased and the other half were unchanged. In only a couple of cases did trade with non-subject countries drop. It is instructive to look at the results in those cases which had significant effects of either the investigation or the withdrawn petition.

Case 438, limousines from Canada, shows an increasing quantity of trade and decreasing price throughout the time period. Case number 496, shopping carts from Taiwan, shows a similar pattern, although there is a drop in price and quantity during the month the case was under investigation, a possible investigation effect.

In terms of potential investigation effects the only case that show a decrease in quantity or an increase in price during the investigation period is cordage from Portugal, case 631. This case, as described on Table I, is one of the cordage cases. The certain cordage products cases were filed three separate times between November 1992 and July 1993. In case 631 there was a decrease in the quantity of trade during the eight months of investigation, but not after the case was withdrawn. While this is the only case with an investigation effect, the cordage cases had the longest investigations in this data set, given the number of somewhat consecutive filings.

Case number 686, steel wire rod from Belgium, prices and quantities increase between the pre-investigation period, the investigation period, and the year after withdrawal. This pattern does not show up in any of the other import equations. Case number 767, ultra high temperature milk from Canada, shows increased price and increased quantity throughout the period. There are few imports of ultra high temperature milk from the rest of the world to the United States and so the rest of world demand equation was not estimated for this case. These are the two cases which show effects which would be potentially consistent with an anticompetitive settlement.

The simple regressions also showed that cases 686 and 767 had either a decrease in quantity or increase in price after the petition was withdrawn relative to before the petition was filed. The market share of subject imports to total imports of a given product, mentioned earlier, is important in this context as well. On average the subject imports in this dataset are 30 percent of total imports for a given product. However, there is a great deal of variance in the market shares. The two cases that showed an increase in price after the petitions were withdrawn have two of the top four market shares of subject imports to total imports. This is consistent with the argument that other imports are significant alternative choices for U.S. buyers and constrain U.S. producers and producers in subject countries. It also raises the issue of examining importer market shares before making generalization about the possibility of collusion.

VI. CONCLUSIONS

The main purpose of this paper was to assess whether the detailed trade data supported the notion that a withdrawn AD petition is a signal that a collusive agreement between domestic and foreign firms had been reached. Economic researchers have accepted as conventional wisdom that withdrawn petitions are a signal of a collusive out-of-court settlement to an AD case. This has progressed to a point where they are being referred to as "settled cases" and lumped together with cases where there has been an suspension agreement or a voluntary export restraint. Models have been designed to ascertain when firms might want to negotiate a collusive settlement with the foreign firms and withdraw their AD petition. It was also claimed, that these out-of-court settlements are legal as well.

Based on the results of this paper both of these beliefs are open to serious question. The data and analysis presented in this paper concerning cases that were withdrawn without a known settlement, i.e. suspension agreement or voluntary export restraint, suggests that out-of-court collusive settlements are not common - at least not in the 1990s. The vast majority of cases saw an increase or no change in the amount of trade. Only in two of the 16 cases did prices increase or quantities decrease. In addition, none of the six cases that only had value data showed a significant decrease in trade. Given the length of time between filing the case and the withdrawal, in a large percentage of cases this is two months, it is likely that a larger percentage of cases are withdrawn because it became clear that they were unlikely to be successful. The results presented in this paper clearly show that it is important to examine price and quantity data not just the value of trade when looking at the impact of trade restraints.

It is important to point out that in the few cases where the trade data showed a decrease in trade or an increase in prices, there are a number of factors which could explain these movements other than collusion. In other words a decrease in the quantity of trade or an increase in price are necessary but not sufficient indicia of collusion. It is useful to note that the simple event regressions gave very similar results to the more fully specified model.

Given the results from this dataset, that withdrawn cases do not seem the result of collusive settlements, a fruitful area for research concerns the development of theoretical models of when firms might want to withdraw cases. The explanation might concern a firm wanting to preserve the threat of future trade protection. A second possible avenue for research would be to look for more sophisticated explanation of collusion. This would include collusive arrangements that come out of successful cases, such as the ferrosilicon case, or potential collusive information exchange in the filing process.

WORKS CITED

American Bar Association, 1997, Antitrust Law Developments, fourth edition.

Calvani, T., Tritell, R.W., 1986, Invocation of United States Import Relief Laws as an Antitrust Violation, Antitrust Bulletin 31, 527--550.

Carey, C. , 1997, U.S. Import Supply Behavior: Evidence from the 1980's, Eastern Economic Journal, 23, 139–149.

Gallaway, M., Blonigen B., Flynn, J., 1999, Welfare costs of the U.S. Antidumping and Countervailing Duty Laws, Journal of International Economics 49, 211--244.

Goldberg, P.K., Knetter, M.M., 1999, Measuring the Intensity of Competition in Export Markets, Journal of International Economics, 47, 27–60.

Goldstein, M., Khan, M., 1978, The Supply and Demand for Exports: A Simultaneous Approach, Review of Economics and Statistics, 60, 275–286.

Harrison, A., 1991, The New Trade Protection: Price Effects of Antidumping and Countervailing Measures in the United States, World Bank Policy Research Working Paper 808.

Hartigan, J.C., Perry, P.R., Kamma, S., 1986, The Value of Administered Protection: A Capital Market Approach, Review of Economics and Statistics, 68, 610--617.

Hartigan, J.C., Sreenivas K., Perry P.R., 1989, The Injury Determination Category and the Value of Relief from Dumping, Review of Economics and Statistics, 71, 183--186.

Herander, M., Schwartz J.B., 1984, An Empirical Test of the Impact of the Threat of U.S. Trade Policy: The Case of Antidumping Duties, Southern Economic Journal, 51, 59--79.

Kalt, J. P., 1988, The Political Economy of Protectionism: Tariffs and Retaliation in the Timber Industry, in Baldwin, R.E.(Ed.) Trade Policy Issues and Empirical Analysis, Chicago: University of Chicago Press, 339--364.

Kennedy, P.E., 1981, Estimation with Correctly Interpreted Dummy Variables in Semilogarithmic Equations, American Economic Review, 71, 802.

Krupp, C., Pollard P.S., 1996, Market Responses to Antidumping Laws: Some Evidence from the U.S. Chemical Industry, Canadian Journal of Economics, 29, 199--227.

Lenway, S., Rehbein K., Starks, L., 1990, The Impact of Protection on Firm Wealth: The Experience of the Steel Industry, Southern Economic Journal, 56, 1079--1093.

Messerlin, P., 1989, The EC Antidumping Regulations: A First Economic Appraisal, 1980-85, Weltwirtschaftliches Archiv, 125, 563--587.

Morkre, M.E., Kelly K. H., 1994, Effects of Unfair Imports on Domestic Industry: U.S. Antidumping and Countervailing Duty Cases, 1980-1988, FTC Bureau of Economics Staff Report.

Pierce, R.. J., 2000, Antidumping Law as a Means of Facilitating Cartelization, Antitrust Law Journal, 67, 725--743.

Prusa, T. J., 1992, Why Are So Many Antidumping Petitions Withdrawn?, Journal of International Economics, 33, 1--20.

Prusa, T. J., 1997, The Trade Effects of U.S. Antidumping Actions, in Robert C. Feenstra (Ed.) The Effects of U.S. Trade Protection and Promotion Policies, Chicago: University of Chicago Press, 191--213.

Prusa, T. J., 1999, On the Spread and Impact of Antidumping, NBER Working Paper No. 7404.

Rosendorf, P.B., 1996, Voluntary Export Restraints, Antidumping Procedure, and Domestic Politics, American Economic Review, 86, 544--561.

Staiger, R.W., F.,A. Wolak, 1994, Measuring Industry Specific Protection: Antidumping in the United States, in Baily, M.N., Reiss, P.C.,Winston C. (Eds.) Brookings Papers on Economic Activity: Microeconomics, Washington D.C.: The Brookings Institution, 51--118.

Thursby, J., Thursby, M.,1984, How Reliable are Simple, Single Equation Specifications of Import Demand?, Review of Economics and Statistics, 66, 120–128.

U.S. Department of Justice and Federal Trade Commission, 1995, Antitrust Enforcement Guidelines for International Operations.

USITC, 1995, The Economic Effects of Antidumping and Countervailing Duty Orders and Suspension Agreements, Publication 2900.

USITC, 1999a, Ferrosilicon from Brazil, China, Kazakhstan, Russia, Ukraine, and Venezuela, Investigation 751-TA-21-27, Publication 3218.

USITC, 1999b, Antidumping and Countervailing Duty Handbook, Publication 3380.

Zanardi, M., 2000, Antidumping Law as a Collusive Device, Boston College Working Paper No. 487.

Table I: Cases Covered in the Analysis:

Product	Case Number	Subject Country	Initiation Date	Termination Date
Cases with value and quantity data:				
Portable Seismographs	731-313	Canada	1992: M2	1992: M6
Limousines	731-438	Canada	1989: M8	1990: M3
Benzyl Paraben	731-463	United Kingdom	1990: M7	1990: M7
Shopping Carts	731-495	China	1991: M1	1991: M1
	731-496	Taiwan	1991: M1	1991: M1
Bulk Ibuprofen	731-526	India	1991: M8	1992: M3
Sulfur Dyes	731-549	Hong Kong	1992: M4	1992: M5
Hairbrushes	731-623	China	1992: M9	1992: M9
Certain Cordage Products	731-628	Costa Rica	1992: M11	1992: M12
	731-629	South Korea	1992: M11	1992: M12
	731-630	Mexico	1992: M11	1992: M12
	731-631	Portugal	1992: M11	1992: M12
Certain Cordage Products	731-632	Costa Rica	1992: M12	1993: M1
	731-633	South Korea	1992: M12	1993: M1
	731-634	Mexico	1992: M12	1993: M1
	731-635	Portugal	1992: M12	1993: M1
Certain Cordage Products	731-654	Costa Rica	1993: M7	1993: M8
	731-655	South Korea	1993: M7	1993: M8
	731-656	Mexico	1993: M7	1993: M8
	731-657	Portugal	1993: M7	1993: M8
Steel Wire Rod	731-647	Canada	1993: M2	1994: M6
Stainless Steel Pipe Fittings	731-658	Taiwan	1993: M8	1994: M7
Steel Wire Rod	731-686	Belgium	1994: M2	1994: M6
Ultra High Temperature Milk	731-767	Canada	1997: M3	1997: M3
Cases with only value data:				
Phototypesetting Machines	731-456	Germany	1990: M3	1990: M10
Woodwind Keypads	731-626	Italy	1992: M9	1992: M9
Wheel Inserts	731-720	China	1994: M9	1994: M10
Drawer Slides	731-723	China	1994: M10	1995: M10
PVC Framing Stock	731-738	United Kingdom	1995: M9	1996: M11

Table II: Simple Regressions on Value, Quantity and Unit Values

Case #	Value		Value	Quantity		Quantity	Unit Values		Unit Values
	Year Before (1)	Year After (2)	(1)-(2)	Year Before (3)	Year After (4)	(3)-(4)	Year Before (5)	Year After (6)	(5)-(6)
ALL	11.73* (0.35)	11.92* (0.34)	-0.19** (0.13)	12.13* (0.32)	12.39* (0.32)	-0.26* (0.13)	-0.40* (0.10)	-0.50* (0.10)	0.10* (0.05)
313	11.04* (0.17)	10.95* (0.17)	0.09 (0.24)	2.67* (0.20)	3.15* (0.20)	-0.48* (0.28)	8.37* (0.20)	7.80* (0.20)	0.57* (0.29)
438	19.55* (0.16)	20.55* (0.13)	-1.00* (0.21)	9.93* (0.19)	11.10* (0.15)	-1.18* (0.24)	9.63* (0.04)	9.45* (0.03)	0.18* (0.04)
463	11.43* (0.31)	11.38* (0.31)	0.05 (0.44)	8.55* (0.63)	8.68* (0.63)	-0.13 (0.89)	2.88* (0.34)	2.70* (0.34)	0.18 (0.48)
495	14.20* (0.07)	14.31* (0.07)	-0.11 (0.09)	11.78* (0.06)	11.91* (0.06)	-0.13 (0.08)	2.41* (0.04)	2.40* (0.04)	0.01 (0.06)
496	12.46* (0.10)	12.87* (0.10)	-0.41* (0.14)	10.34* (0.11)	10.89* (0.11)	-0.54* (0.16)	2.12* (0.04)	1.99* (0.04)	0.13* (0.05)
526	12.58* (1.21)	10.31* (1.21)	2.27 (1.72)	9.90* (0.15)	8.05* (0.96)	1.85 (1.35)	2.68* (0.01)	2.71* (0.01)	-0.03* (0.01)
549	6.07* (1.55)	5.41* (1.55)	0.66 (2.20)	4.83* (1.37)	5.00* (1.37)	-0.17 (1.94)	2.12* (0.44)	0.82 (0.47)	1.31** (0.64)
623	14.06* (0.07)	14.41* (0.07)	-0.35* (0.10)	15.16* (0.05)	15.51* (0.05)	-0.35* (0.07)	-1.10* (0.04)	-1.10* (0.04)	0.01 (0.06)
628	9.91* (0.57)	11.63* (0.57)	-1.72* (0.81)	9.48* (0.57)	11.52* (0.57)	-2.04* (0.81)	0.47* (0.13)	0.12 (0.13)	0.36** (0.18)
629	13.07* (0.08)	13.58* (0.09)	-0.51* (0.13)	12.38* (0.08)	12.64* (0.08)	-0.26* (0.11)	0.70* (0.13)	0.94* (0.13)	-0.25 (0.18)
630	13.01* (0.09)	13.80* (0.10)	-0.78* (0.10)	11.76* (0.13)	12.31* (0.13)	-0.54* (0.18)	1.31* (0.06)	1.28* (0.06)	0.04 (0.09)
631	11.02* (0.16)	11.58* (0.16)	-0.56* (0.22)	8.89* (0.20)	9.58* (0.20)	-0.68* (0.29)	2.13* (0.14)	2.00* (0.04)	0.14 (0.20)
647	10.32* (0.14)	10.93* (0.14)	-0.61* (0.19)	10.79* (0.26)	11.19* (0.26)	-0.40 (0.37)	0.47* (0.17)	-0.26 (0.17)	-0.21 (0.24)
658	14.29* (0.08)	14.30* (0.08)	-0.00 (0.11)	12.05* (0.09)	12.07* (0.09)	-0.02 (0.12)	2.24* (0.04)	2.22* (0.04)	0.02 (0.06)
686	16.66* (0.04)	16.64* (0.04)	0.02 (0.06)	17.57* (0.04)	17.45* (0.04)	0.11** (0.06)	-0.91* (0.01)	-0.81* (0.01)	-0.10* (0.02)
767	11.20* (0.75)	12.39* (0.75)	-1.19 (1.06)	11.72* (0.78)	12.74* (0.78)	-1.02 (1.11)	-0.57* (0.02)	-0.25* (0.02)	-0.22* (0.03)

* - Significant at the 5% level
** - Significant at the 10% level

Table III: Simple Regressions on Values

Case	Values Year Before (1)	Year After (2)	Values (1)-(2)
456	6.38* (0.04)	6.34* (0.04)	0.04 (0.06)
626	5.10* (0.04)	5.09* (0.04)	0.01 (0.06)
720	5.63* (0.06)	5.75* (0.06)	-0.12 (0.08)
723	5.63* (0.03)	6.02* (0.03)	-0.40* (0.05)
738	5.78* (0.05)	5.93* (0.05)	-0.15* (0.07)

* - Significant at the 5% level
** - Significant at the 10% level

Table IV - Price and Quantity Effects of Terminated Dumping and Countervailing Duty Cases

Case	Price of Subject			Quantity of Subject			Quantity of All Other			Price of Subject			Quantity of Subject			Quantity of Non-Subject		
	Year Before (1)	Inv. (2)	Year After (3)	Year Before (4)	Inv. (5)	Year After (6)	Year Before (7)	Inv. (8)	Year After (9)	Subject (1)-(2)	Subject (1)-(3)	Subject (2)-(3)	Subject (4)-(5)	Subject (4)-(6)	Subject (5)-(6)	All Other (7)-(8)	All Other (7)-(9)	All Other (8)-(9)
313	-0.38* (0.16)	-0.56* (0.23)	-0.50* (0.16)	-0.22 (0.22)	-0.17 (0.33)	0.20 (0.34)	-0.42 (0.37)	-0.30 (0.52)	-0.90* (0.36)	0.18 (0.24)	0.11 (0.19)	-0.07 (0.24)	-0.06 (0.32)	-0.43 (0.33)	-0.37 (0.32)	-0.12 (0.53)	0.48 (0.41)	0.60 (0.53)
438	3.44 (2.95)	3.31 (2.90)	2.98 (2.76)	16.89* (4.36)	17.23* (4.31)	17.77* (4.25)	-1.98 (4.35)	-1.25 (4.33)	-0.05 (4.26)	0.13 (0.09)	0.46** (0.26)	0.33** (0.19)	-0.33* (0.11)	-0.88* (0.15)	-0.54* (0.10)	-0.73* (0.13)	-1.93* (0.22)	-1.20* (0.17)
463	0.19 (0.34)	0.13 (0.67)	0.13 (0.32)	-1.81 (1.88)	-1.99 (4.71)	-1.40 (1.89)	-0.56* (0.27)	0.71 (0.69)	-0.23 (0.27)	0.06 (0.75)	0.06 (0.18)	0.00 (0.73)	0.18 (4.90)	-0.41 (1.47)	-0.59 (4.80)	-1.28** (0.73)	-0.33** (0.20)	0.95 (0.72)
495	0.05 (0.15)	-0.15 (0.49)	0.15 (0.16)	0.22 (0.14)	0.49** (0.29)	0.38* (0.19)	-0.26* (0.08)	-0.67* (0.21)	-0.07 (0.08)	0.20 (0.45)	-0.10 (0.14)	-0.30 (0.45)	-0.27 (0.26)	-0.16 (0.11)	0.11 (0.25)	0.41* (0.20)	-0.19* (0.08)	-0.60* (0.21)
496	-0.15* (0.05)	-0.41* (0.11)	-0.29* (0.11)	0.43* (0.20)	0.36 (0.55)	1.22* (0.25)	-0.85* (0.22)	-2.31* (0.65)	-1.46 (0.38)	0.27* (0.11)	0.15* (0.08)	-0.12 (0.15)	0.07 (0.52)	-0.80* (0.20)	-0.87** (0.49)	1.47* (0.48)	0.61* (0.20)	-0.86* (0.34)
526	0.00 (0.06)	0.00 (0.06)	0.00 (0.04)	-0.07 (0.33)	-0.05 (0.63)	-0.56 (0.71)	-1.17* (0.31)	0.12 (0.35)	0.85* (0.29)	-0.03 (0.05)	-0.03 (0.06)	0.00 (0.07)	-0.02 (0.50)	0.50 (0.55)	0.52 (0.37)	-1.30* (0.37)	-2.02* (0.32)	-0.73* (0.36)
549	-0.35 (0.67)	-0.25 (0.82)	-0.32 (0.32)	0.03 (0.58)	-2.01 (1.46)	-1.26 (1.14)	-0.14 (0.19)	0.67** (0.38)	0.47* (0.15)	-0.10 (1.35)	-0.03 (0.71)	0.07 (0.85)	2.04 (1.47)	1.29 (1.14)	-0.75 (1.00)	-0.81 (0.51)	-0.61* (0.27)	0.19 (0.34)
623	-0.02 (0.07)	-0.16 (0.13)	-0.07 (0.08)	0.66* (0.12)	0.74* (0.35)	0.88** (0.13)	0.06 (0.14)	0.23 (0.41)	-0.05 (0.22)	0.14 (0.13)	0.05 (0.05)	-0.09 (0.13)	-0.09 (0.35)	-0.22** (0.13)	-0.14 (0.35)	-0.17 (0.34)	0.11 (0.14)	0.28 (0.28)
628	-0.01 (0.14)	0.05 (0.39)	0.37 (0.83)	-1.67* (0.73)	-0.06 (0.76)	0.43 (0.76)	-0.09 (0.04)	-0.06 (0.06)	0.43 (0.76)	-0.05 (0.39)	-0.38 (0.82)	-0.33 (0.49)	-1.61* (0.81)	-2.10* (0.75)	-0.49 (0.75)	-0.32 (0.07)	-0.09 (0.07)	-0.56 (0.05)

* - Significant at the 5% level
** - Significant at the 10% level

Table IV - Price and Quantity Effects of Terminated Dumping and Countervailing Duty Cases (cont.)

Case	Price of Subject			Quantity of Subject			Quantity of All Other			Price of Subject			Quantity of Subject			Quantity of Non-Subject		
	Year Before (1)	Inv. (2)	Year After (3)	Year Before (4)	Inv. (5)	Year After (6)	Year Before (7)	Inv. (8)	Year After (9)	Subject (1)-(2)	Subject (1)-(3)	Subject (2)-(3)	Subject (4)-(5)	Subject (4)-(6)	Subject (5)-(6)	All Other (7)-(8)	All Other (7)-(9)	All Other (8)-(9)
629	0.10 (0.17)	-0.07 (0.15)	-0.16 (0.15)	-0.17* (0.07)	-0.06 (0.09)	0.20* (0.10)	-0.05 (0.04)	0.02 (0.04)	0.09** (0.05)	0.18 (0.18)	0.26 (0.21)	0.09 (0.17)	-0.22* (0.09)	-0.37* (0.09)	-0.15** (0.09)	-0.05 (0.05)	-0.14* (0.06)	-0.08** (0.05)
630	-0.09 (0.07)	-0.13 (0.09)	-0.25* (0.09)	-0.19 (0.14)	-0.07* (0.15)	0.16 (0.16)	-0.12 (0.08)	-0.09 (0.10)	-0.08 (0.15)	0.04 (0.09)	0.16** (0.09)	0.11 (0.10)	-0.12 (0.16)	-0.34* (0.15)	-0.22 (0.16)	-0.03 (0.07)	-0.04 (0.11)	-0.01 (0.10)
631	-0.23** (0.12)	-0.26** (0.15)	0.06 (0.14)	-0.14 (0.25)	-0.63* (0.26)	-0.22 (0.26)	-0.30** (0.18)	-0.32 (0.20)	-0.12 (0.21)	0.03 (0.17)	-0.30** (0.16)	-0.33* (0.16)	0.49** (0.29)	0.08 (0.35)	-0.41 (0.30)	0.02 (0.19)	-0.42 (0.28)	-0.44 (0.28)
647	0.05 (0.18)	0.11 (0.27)	0.28 (0.20)	0.90 (2.83)	1.80 (4.54)	4.25 (4.40)	0.43* (0.07)	0.44* (0.10)	0.56* (0.13)	-0.06 (0.30)	-0.23 (0.23)	-0.17 (0.30)	-0.90 (4.66)	-3.35 (4.30)	-2.45 (4.71)	-0.01 (0.09)	-0.13 (0.11)	-0.12 (0.11)
658	-0.01 (0.04)	-0.01 (0.07)	-0.01 (0.11)	0.09 (0.13)	-0.05 (0.11)	0.11 (0.13)	-0.22* (0.08)	0.05 (0.12)	0.23 (0.18)	-0.00 (0.06)	0.00 (0.09)	0.01 (0.07)	0.13 (0.14)	-0.02 (0.13)	-0.16 (0.14)	-0.27* (0.11)	-0.45* (0.15)	-0.17 (0.12)
686	0.17* (0.04)	0.14* (0.04)	0.25* (0.04)	0.61* (0.10)	0.82* (0.44)	1.17* (0.29)	0.31* (0.09)	0.24 (0.17)	0.23 (0.21)	0.03 (0.05)	-0.08* (0.04)	-0.10* (0.05)	-0.21 (0.18)	-0.56* (0.22)	-0.35* (0.13)	0.07 (0.13)	0.08 (0.15)	0.01 (0.12)
767	0.09 (0.14)	0.21 (0.33)	0.30 (0.21)	1.92 (1.52)	4.23 (4.10)	5.80* (1.74)	NA	NA	NA	-0.13 (0.30)	-0.22** (0.14)	-0.10 (0.30)	-2.32 (4.08)	-3.88* (1.61)	-1.57 (4.09)	NA	NA	NA

* - Significant at the 5% level
** - Significant at the 10% level
NA - Not Applicable